NYUM BAI!

A CAMBODIAN COOKBOOK

the green gecko

Have you eaten?

Nyum Bai?

'Nyum Bai' is one of the most soulful words in the Khmer language, it is both an invitation and an inquiry Lets eat! Or have you eaten? It literally translates to 'eat rice' - whether it's breakfast, lunch or dinner, the question is always the same... no matter if there is rice involved or not.

Nyum Bai? is asked with a beaming face... this signature conversational line exudes genuine Khmer warmth and hospitality, something we hear a lot of at Green Gecko.

Take a stroll along any main road in a typical Cambodian city and you can sample crickets, beetles or even spiders - the perfect afternoon snack for a Cambodian who wants fast food that is high in nutrients and protein! The favourite way to eat them is deep fried and is the equivalent to eating popcorn or nuts. During the rainy season the vibrating sound of frogs can be heard everywhere. They make a good meal too!

About the GREEN GECKO Project

The GREEN GECKO Project is an initiative founded to benefit the lives of street children in Siem Reap, Cambodia. A recently emerging town located in the north-west of the country, it is home to the world's largest religious site 'Angkor Wat' and consequently, a hastily growing tourism industry.

In the past, any tourist strolling along the streets of Siem Reap would have come across these children. While most would have certainly been hassled by their begging, not many would have had the pleasure of getting to know the kids themselves - their humour, tenacity, resourcefulness, hope, trust and friendship. The GREEN GECKO Project began when one tourist took the time to do this in 2005.

The sad reality then was that these children, as young as 5 years old, were often the primary breadwinners for their families. Their living conditions were often desperate, either living in very poor housing or no housing at all. Some of the children slept unaccompanied on the pavement, defenceless to abduction, abuse and disease.

Thankfully, today we can describe these terrible conditions in the past tense, at least for the children we have been able to reach out to. The GREEN GECKO Project now supports children that are ex-beggars! 97% of our kids are off the streets completely and all kids of school age are now attending accredited Khmer school.

The GREEN GECKO Project is about empowering these children with skills, education, care and support to enable them to break the begging cycle and live to their highest potential.

At GREEN GECKO, the children can eat 3 meals per day, attend an English class, feel secure, play, get a hug, put their pictures up on the wall, have a shower, get their hair combed, nails cut, brush their teeth and receive regula medical checkups.

ey can attend fun excursions and receive the chance to expand their
erests and knowledge of new subjects, by participating (somewhat
husiastically) in dance, art and craft, drama, gymnastics and performance
sses.

ne of the most significant recent additions is a night shelter which now
uses over two thirds of the children. There are three shelters; one for the
ys, one for the girls and one for the toddlers. Each has a permanent house
rent staying with them, keeping them safe and secure, sometimes for the
t time in their very short lives.

as been a long and difficult task to convince the kids' parents that
ucation and recreation for their child is a worthwhile investment. The
ldren could be out making money and the parents, either hungry or with
diction problems, have little concept of a future beyond their immediate
eds. This has come about as most of these parents have lived through the
ocities of the Khmer Rouge and many are landmine amputees with little
ucation or opportunities. Experience has already proved that supporting
d connecting with these families is essential to the success of the project.
REEN GECKO has steadily gained parent approval and some now are
en actively encouraging their children to learn.

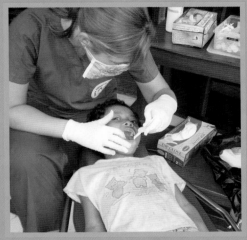

e November 2006 crackdown on begging in Siem Reap had varied effects
GREEN GECKO. We shared the same aim, to get the kids off the street
t unfortunately it also left the families without any source of income at all.
ing to ward off even less desirable ways of surviving, the GREEN GECKO
oject sponsored (with the help of their friends) the development of micro
sinesses for many of the families. Book stalls, noodle stands and fruit carts,
en a stall that sells sautéed snails… are some of the successful businesses.

hough we know we have a long way to go, we are grateful and
erwhelmed by the support and the results already received and achieved.

July 2007, the GREEN GECKO Project became a registered NGO in
ambodia and on the 16th August 2007, we signed a 15 year lease on 1¼
res of land. So while we are very proud of how far the kids have come, we
e even more excited about the potential of their future and that of our new
ome. With new classrooms to build, playgrounds to make and gardens to
ant, we certainly have our hands full, but with continued support moral,
ysical and financial - we are sure that the difference we are making for
ese kids will spill over to future generations.

My name is Kom Suan, I am 12 years old.

Before, I was a begging child on the streets I carried my baby sister and begged for money I felt sad and many times I wanted to cry. I felt like I had finished my energy.

I love my Mum and Dad but I did not like them drinking beer and playing cards they would hit me and my sisters to beg more.

When I was 9 years old, I met Tania. She gave us food every night and was very kind but we thought she would go back to her country soon. She did not go back. Tania met Rem and they got married. They took us to English School and soon started Green Gecko. At this time I felt so happy and wanted to learn so much. They also helped my family to stop begging and gave them a business. I felt so proud about that.

I live at Green Gecko now and see my parents every week. We get lots of food, care and love. The doctor comes, we play games and learn computers. All of the children feel so happy and so lucky. Before, I had no idea about my future but I knew I did not want to be like other girls and go with men for money. This is a very bad life and sometimes girls don't come back.

I hope that Cambodia has no more war, people are kind to each other and there is enough food to eat. For me I want to be a good student and become a teacher who will help others stop begging so they can change their lives… just like me.

For the first time, I feel excited about my life.

My name is Kom Suan. Thank you for reading my story.

Bon Ton

I want to be a tourist guide, have a wife, house and 3 kids, but for now I would like jeans, a DJ hat and to stay in school.

Saron

I want to be a doctor so I can help Green Gecko children when they get sick.

Thy

My dream is to go to Shinta Mani so I can become a cook. When I save my money I want to help the poor children of Cambodia, just like Rem.

Srey Neang

Education is my life. When I grow up I would like to be an English teacher so I can pay three months rent for my parents and give them food to eat.

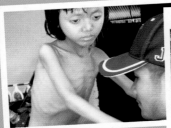

Sunly

I love Tania and I love Rem. I love Green Gecko. I can sing the ABC and rainbow song.

7

How GREEN GECKO began...

Responding to an article she read in a Virgin in-flight magazine, Australian born Tania Palmer walked off the plane and into a travel agency to book a flight. The Article was about an orphanage in need. The destination was Siem Reap, Cambodia. The date was August 2004.

A month later, Tania, co-director of hugabub.com - a baby sling company located in Byron Bay, Australia - found herself among the stifling heat and humidity with eyes, arms and heart wide open to the plight of the Cambodian children.

Soon after, she was back home, in body but not in spirit. By February 2005, Tania had packed up her life, home and office desk to return to Cambodia. No plan, no goal and no idea of what the future would bring. She described 'the calling' as being so strong that it defied all reasonable logic.

In the meantime Rem Poum was a Siem Reap tuk tuk driver "I wanted to be a driver for a long time because I wanted to support my family. I wanted to help my brother and sister to study so they could get a good job and help my family in the future, so I could become a monk" Rem said.

The children had stolen Tania's heart and so had this lovely local man named Rem, who was soon to be Tania's husband and the other half of the GREEN GECKO team. Rem's plans of monk hood were over.

While Tania's attentions were immediately drawn towards the street kids, Rem was surprised at her willingness to help. "When I saw Tania wanting to help them I asked myself 'what am I?' then I say 'I am a Cambodian man and this is Cambodia'. I decided I wanted to help the children too and then the good luck came and we fell in love".

Beggar children, who were often tiny themselves, were laden with babies on their hips in slings to attract more sympathy and... more money from wealthy foreign tourists. The children never held onto money for long, they would hand it to their families. Tania and Rem wanted to help, wanted to give them something that could not be taken away from them. The answer was food.

What started as a single table of six on the pavement at a local restaurant grew to many tables being joined together to feed sometimes more than 30 street children. Sadly the prejudices towards the children by their own people, made it more and more difficult to find places for them to dine. Besides that, Tania says "feeding the kids on a nightly basis was one thing; it was nice to know their bellies were full, but it was not really contributing to their future. We wanted to provide them with fishing rods, not just the fish". So with these two factors in mind, Tania and Rem decided the only sensible solution was to find a place where the children could learn and eat without people shooing them out of sight.

They approached a local English school and asked if they could pay for the children to go to the school. They refused on the basis the children were dirty, stinky and noisy and that the parents of 'normal' children would not like it if they were in the same class. Despite the truth of the comments, it was, unknowingly, the catalyst that planted the seed for the GREEN GECKO Project. Their answer was to start a class of their own.

What started as a small token gesture to get the children off the streets for an hour or two turned out to be more successful than they imagined. The children enthusiastically participated in learning English and enjoyed the hot meal they received after class. However with success came limitations; there was no running water, nowhere to wash, eat properly, brush teeth or receive medical treatment... not even a place to just hang out and play.

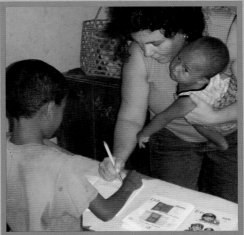

After three months of high attendance and dedication, it was time for the next step. On 1 October 2005, a small ex-police station was leased, which looked exactly like a schoolhouse. The children moved in the next day, elated with their new abode. The doors opened with no teacher, no resources, no desks, no chairs, no mats and no whiteboard. What the kids had though was a place they could feel safe and call their own - a place to play and learn. They also had a shower, toilet and running water. It was a place where the children beamed with pride, passion and enthusiasm.

Rem and I are strong believers that with the right intention you can make things happen, and for the Gecko, the ball just keeps rolling. The response from the beginning has been amazing, absolutely overwhelming. Out of seemingly nowhere has come an abundance of specialised volunteers, advice, support and brilliant ideas. We could not have achieved so much in so little time without the generosity of others with continued support our goals and dreams seem all the more achievable".

Cooking Cambodian Style

Cambodian cooking has a rich and diverse cultural history, and most recipes are straight-forward and delicious! The ideal Cambodian meal is a harmonious blend of fresh ingredients balanced together to bring out colours, aromas, spices and herbs.

A typical traditional Cambodian meal consists of soup, salad, meats, vegetable dishes and rice. Meals are most often served with the main dishes placed in the centre of table (or a mat) each person has a bowl of rice and everybody digs is in!

Dishes are not chosen randomly, but are designed to compliment each other, balancing flavours and textures; they look great and taste even better. Delicious sauces and condiments are served with the meal to add extra flavour, and in some cases extra spices.

The method of Cambodian cooking is short and simple and recipes are passed down from generation to generation. Unfortunately, many secret family recipes were lost during the years of the Khmer Rouge.

Generally Khmer people take the eating portion of the meal quite seriously and get into it without a lot of conversation but Cambodia's strong family and community spirit means that eating is a shared celebration whether it is sitting together on the floor at home or meeting friends at an outdoor café.

Influences

Stirfrying is very popular with the locals creating a quick dish consisting of noodles, meat and vegetables, often cooked in a sauce made from a fish base or shrimp paste. The fish sauce is often diluted with water, and after a little red chilli has been added for taste, it makes a great dipping sauce for meat or vegetable skewers and fresh spring rolls.

The French occupation of Cambodia in the early twentieth century left its mark on the local cuisine. Frogs legs are still popular, waffles & pastries are a favourite and baguettes are sold by most street vendors.

Typical Ingredients

The most essential ingredient in most Khmer dishes is an aromatic and pungent paste known as 'kroeung', a mix of dried chilli, lemongrass, kafir lime leaves, galangal, turmeric, garlic and fish sauce. It's a must for most curries and stirfry dishes.

The most unique Cambodian ingredient is 'prahok', a fermented fish paste that not only for its distinct and overbearing flavour but it has an aroma that would rival the most pungent of edibles. It's distinctly Cambodian and its potency should not be underestimated, apply with caution!

Like most curry dishes found around the world, coconut milk or coconut cream plays a large part in creating the correct consistency and sweetness of the sauce, and coconut 'water' as they call it here is a trusted remedy for a lingering fever.

Banana blossom, lotus roots, and green mango make a good basis for a light and refreshing salad, and are ingredients that are abundant in Cambodia.

A magnificent flower and representing an ancient symbol, the lotus plant is also used widely in cooking. Once you peel away the petals, the seeds have a slight nutty flavour. The lotus root when cleaned, peeled and sliced resembles little snowflakes that are generously added to stir-fry's and salads.

Cambodian cuisine contains very little fat, making it one of the world's tastiest and healthiest cuisines and perhaps a contributing factor to the lithe physiques of the locals.

We hope while you cook your way through this book, you allow your sense of adventure, imagination, instinct and taste buds to take control.

Som pesa dowie ric re-ay (please enjoy)!

VEGETARIAN

Due to the cost of meat, many Cambodians live mainly on a diet of vegetables, fruit, and rice, with fish as an occasional supplement.

Vegetarian meals are an integral part of the daily diet and the plethora of fresh vegetables, fruit, nuts, rice, noodles and herbs, always ensure a delicious selection of salads, soups and stirfries.

VEGETARIAN FRIED SPRING ROLLS
Bunlay Chayor Bompong

These delectable little crispy rolls are ideal as both a starter or snack. If you can't get spring roll wrappers, this recipe will also work using filo pastry as a substitute. **Makes 20 pieces.**

Ingredients

20 sheets spring roll wrappers
2 cups mushrooms, finely diced
½ cup bean sprouts
½ cup shredded cabbage
½ cup shredded carrots
1 egg beaten
1 cup clear rice noodles, soaked and drained

3 cloves of garlic, chopped
½ teaspoon salt
½ teaspoon sugar
1 teaspoon sweet chilli sauce
pinch of black pepper

How to prepare

1. Lightly fry the garlic in a little oil for about 5 minutes, stirring constantly to ensure the garlic does not burn.

2. Add the carrots and cabbage and cook for a further 3 minutes. Toss into the pan the mushrooms & bean sprouts for a final 2 minutes.

3. Turn off the heat and mix in clear noodles and the salt, sugar and pepper, then set aside.

4. Place a spoonful of the stir fried mixture on to each spring roll wrapper. Roll up tightly, tucking in the edges and brush with a little egg on the final edge to seal the roll.

5. Deep fry until golden and drain on a paper towel prior to serving.

6. Serve with sweet chilli sauce for dipping and drizzling.

Recommended Beverage

A Chilean fruity light red wine like a Merlot Rose.

MORNING GLORY STIRFRY
Char Bunlay Trokwan

This dish is a crunchy, spicy assembly of vegetables in a light curry sauce. Morning glory is a vegetable indigenous to most of Southeast Asia, and is also known as water spinach. If you can't locate it then spinach makes an ideal substitute.
Serves 4.

Ingredients

1 cup of morning glory or spinach
3 cups red cabbage, sliced
3 cups broccoli florets
1 large onion, sliced
3 cloves garlic, chopped finely
4 medium carrots cut into chunky matchsticks
1 large red capsicum, cut into chunky matchsticks
½ cup vegetable stock
2 red chillies, chopped finely
3 tablespoons chopped fresh mint

3 tablespoons soy sauce
2 teaspoons curry paste
1 teaspoon sugar
1 teaspoon pepper
2 tablespoons vegetable oil

How to prepare

1. Combine curry paste, soy sauce, ½ of the chopped chilli, stock, sugar & pepper and set to one side.

2. Heat 1 tablespoon oil in frypan/wok over medium-high heat. Add onion and garlic and stir fry for about 4 minutes until both are golden brown.

3. Add in broccoli, carrots and capsicum and cook for a further for 3 minutes.

4. Add remaining oil, sauce mixture, morning glory and cabbage.

5. Stir-fry until morning glory & cabbage wilts and vegetables are crisp but tender - about at extra 2 minutes. Remove from the heat and stir in mint.

6. Sprinkle left over chilli on the top and serve as a side dish or with rice.

Recommended Beverage
A Californian dry white wine like a Pinot Grigio

KORKO VEGGIE SOUP
Samlor Ko Khor

Kokor is a traditional thick Khmer soup that really warms you up all over. You can add any vegetables that are in season or for extra interest tofu or any meats.
Serves 4.

Ingredients

2 cups roughly cut up pumpkin
1 cup cabbage, sliced
2 medium sized carrots, sliced
1 large eggplant
20 large long beans, sliced
1 medium onion sliced
2 cloves garlic, minced
1 cup in-season vegetables (etc spinach, capsicum, broccoli)
5 cups vegetable stock (or substitute chicken stock)
¼ cup rice flour
2 tablespoons vegetable oil

1 teaspoon galangal or substitute ginger
½ teaspoon turmeric
1 tablespoon fish sauce
1 teaspoon sugar
½ teaspoon pepper
1 stalk lemongrass

How to prepare

1. Pan fry pumpkin, garlic and onion for about 8 minutes until just soft. Add eggplant and cook for a further 2 minutes.

2. Finely chop and pound the lemongrass and galangal (ginger) into a paste.

3. Combine pepper, lemongrass, turmeric, fish sauce, sugar and galangal.

4. Place all cooked and raw vegetables, spice mix and stock into large deep pot. Cook on high heat for about 15 minutes until vegetables are just cooked. Taste and add more salt/chilli if needed.

5. Add rice flour and stir for no more than 2 minutes until soup thickens. Remove from heat and place into serving dishes and serve immediately.

Recommended Beverage
A Chilean round white wine like a dry crisp Chardonnay

Recipe sponsored by Khmer Kitchen

CARAMELIZED PINEAPPLE & TOFU

Khor Mnoas Tofu

A sauce of caramelized sugar, soy sauce, garlic and black pepper is delicious, very easy to cook and has a beautiful balance of flavours. **Serves 2.**

Ingredients
2 large pieces tofu,
1 cup fresh pineapple,
2 tablespoons vegetarian oyster sauce or mushroom sauce
½ cup water
1 clove garlic, minced.
2 teaspoons soy sauce
2 tablespoons vegetable oil
3 teaspoon sugar
¼ teaspoon salt
¼ teaspoon black pepper
1 stalk green onion, chopped.
A handful of fresh coriander (cilantro) chopped

How to prepare
1. Cut the pieces of tofu and pineapple into bite sized chunks.

2. Place the pineapple, sugar & oil into a hot frypan and stirfry until sugar caramilises for about 4 minutes.

3. Mix the oyster sauce, water, garlic, soy sauce, salt and pepper together.

4. Add the sauce mixture, tofu and green onion into the pan with the caramalised pineapple and cook on medium heat until the water reduces (about 5 minutes)

5. Garnish with coriander and serve hot with rice.

Recommended Beverage
A refreshing light fruity Sauvignon Blanc from Australia's Margaret River region.

STEAMED EGGPLANT
Chamhoy Trop Kdoh Ko

This eggplant dish is a winner, the combination of the garlic, lemongrass and chilli will leave your tastebuds tingling and your stomach pleading for more. **Serves 4.**

Ingredients

2 medium size eggplants
6 cloves garlic, diced finely
2 small red chillies (chopped finely)
2 tablespoons chicken stock
¼ cup of water
2 tablespoons spring onions, chopped
fresh chopped chilli

2 tablespoons vegetable oil
1 teaspoon sugar
2 tablespoons soy sauce
1 teaspoon black pepper
1 teaspoon salt

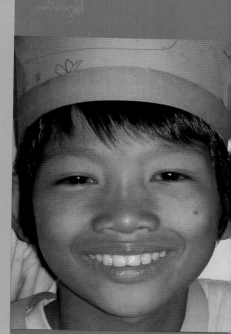

How to prepare

1. Bring 2 cups water to boil in a steamer or large pan in medium oven.

2. Cut the eggplant in ½ inch or ¾ inch slices. Place slices into a dish that will fit into the steamer or pan. Don't worry if slices overlap slightly.

3. Combine the garlic, lemongrass and chillies and spread evenly on top of the eggplant. Combine the oil, sugar, salt, pepper, soy sauce, chicken stock and water together and pour on top of the eggplant.

4. Cover and increase heat until steam comes up through the steamer or/oven. Cook for about 15 minutes, take out and test to see if the eggplant is tender and soft to the touch when a sharp knife is inserted. If not tender, cook for a further 5-10 minutes. Cooking times will vary depending of the type of eggplant used and the thickness of the slices.

5. Serve, garnished with spring onions and fresh chilli

Recommended Beverage
A Spanish mineral white wine containing Rueda Verdejo

FISH & SEAFOOD

In the regions surrounding Tonlé Sap-the huge freshwater lake that dominates the geography of Cambodia - fish and seafood caught from this ecological hotspot are proudly served in a variety of ways, be it in Amok curry, made with coconut milk and fresh basil, or served steamed with fresh vegetables or partnered with lemongrass to make a refreshing soup.

Cambodia is now also cultivating fish farming and is exporting fresh, frozen, smoked and dried fish worldwide.

FISH, LEMONGRASS & BASIL SALAD
Plei Trey

A traditional Cambodian salad that will tantalise your guests with its tangy combination of fresh herbs and spices. You can also substitute the fish for tofu if you would like a refreshing vegetarian dish. **Serves 2.**

Ingredients

2 large fish fillets
2 sliced tomatoes
1 medium sized cucumber
3 carrots, sliced lengthwise
10 long beans, sliced thinly
1 onion, sliced thinly
4 large lettuce leaves
1 fresh red chilli, chopped finely
½ cup roasted peanuts, chopped roughly (optional)

2 tablespoons of vegetable oil
1 teaspoon salt
1 teaspoon sugar
2 tablespoons fresh lime juice
20 basil leaves
1 clove garlic, minced
2 sticks lemongrass, chopped finely

How to prepare

1. Arrange the lettuce leaves onto serving dish and add sliced tomatoes and cucumbers cut into chunky pieces.

2. Combine all other vegetables and basil, mix and add to serving dish.

3. Mix lime juice, salt, sugar, chilli, garlic and lemongrass. Taste and sweeten with sugar or add more chilli according to taste. Set aside.

4. Slice fish into thin fillets (lengthwise) and add the sauce mixture. Pan fry the fish mixture in a little oil until the fish is cooked through (about 2 minutes).

5. Strain the sauce from the fish and pour onto the salad mixture.

6. Layer the fish on the top and sprinkle with peanuts. Serve with steamed brown rice.

Recommended Beverage

A typical French Loire Valley white wine like a Muscadet.

SOUR & SPICY FISH SOUP
Sengao Chrouk Trey

s delicious soup, which has a sweet and tangy flavour, due to the combination of eapple, tamarind and fish sauce, can be made with chicken, prawns or any mixture of food. **Serves 2.**

gredients

nick fillets white fish, cut into cubes	¼ cup basil, chopped
ices pineapple, cut in 1 inch pieces	¼ cup parsley, chopped
up water	1 tablespoon fish sauce
ups vegetable stock	1 teaspoon salt
mall red chilli, sliced	2 tablespoons sugar
cup sawleaf (or spinach), chopped	1 garlic clove, finely chopped

andful bean sprouts
ablespoons vegetable oil
nuckle fresh tamarind (see below) or 2 teaspoons of tamarind paste
ablespoons spring onion, chopped

w to prepare

Heat the oil in a pan. Fry the fish lightly with garlic and chilli for about 4 minutes. The does not have to be completely cooked at this time.

n a pot, bring the vegetable stock & water to a boil. Add fried fish and cook for out 3 minutes, then add in the cabbage.

Add 2 tablespoons of tamarind juice/paste, fish sauce, pineapple, salt and sugar. ust the broth with extra sugar, fish sauce and tamarind juice according to your taste. broth should be a little bit sour, and a little bit sweet.

Turn off the heat and take the pot off the stove. Add basil, bean sprouts and saw leaf. inkle with green onions before serving with rice.

extract the tamarind juice

1 cup of water. Mash the fresh tamarind in warm water. Wait a few minutes for the narind juice to come out. Drain the tamarind seeds and large pulp. Keep only the narind juice.

commended Beverage

Italian light refreshing white wine such as a Grillo di Sicillia.

STEAMED FISH & SOY SAUCE
Trey Chamhoy Teuk Siew

...asy to prepare, hard to mess up, and very versatile - this mouth-watering steamed fish dish is ...easoned with a tangy array of sauces and ginger. **Serves 2.**

Ingredients

medium fish steaks
sprigs of spring onions
½ medium red capsicum
2 long green beans
tablespoon chicken stock
lettuce leaves
0 thinly sliced pieces of fresh ginger
...oriander for garnish
...resh chopped chili on the side

2 tablespoons vegetable oil
2 tablespoons Mirin sauce
4 tablespoons soy sauce
1 tablespoon Teriyaki sauce'
1 teaspoon sugar
1 teaspoon salt
½ cup water

How to prepare

. Bring 2 cups of water to boil in fish poacher or large frypan with a tight fitting lid.

. Place the fish steaks on a greased rack so fish does not touch the water.

. Combine all the soy sauces, oil, water, sugar, salt and stock together. Pour ½ the mixture ...venly over the top of the fish steaks. Keep some aside.

. Chop the spring onions, capsicums, ginger and beans into thin strips and add to the fish.

. Cover pan tightly, steam until fish flakes easily when tested with fork, approx 6 minutes. ...Every two minutes pour a little more of the sauce onto the fish as it cooks.

. Position the lettuce on the bottom of a serving plate and when the fish is cooked, place on ...he top or to the side of the lettuce.

. Garnish with chopped coriander and fresh chili on the side.

Recommended Beverage
...A delicate dry French white wine like a Chardonnay-Terret Pays d' Oc.

Recipe sponsored by Red Orchid

31

TRADITIONAL BBQ SEAFOOD
Ang Trey Samot

hrow table manners to the wind and dig in with your fingers; it's the only way to njoy BBQ Seafood. Use the sauces as either dipping sauces or as a marinade. his recipe can easily be adapted to suit most meats although the cooking times ill have to be adjusted. **Serves 4.**

ngredients
6 large shrimps/prawns
tubes of squid, cleaned & sliced
thick white fish fillets
egetable oil

Chilli Sauce
2 tablespoons fish sauce
1 tablespoon sugar
1 teaspoon ground tamarind
2 cloves garlic, crushed
1 shallot, sliced finely
¼ cup hot water
1 red chilli, sliced

Pepper Sauce
2 tablespoons ground black pepper
1 tablespoon salt
¼ cup fresh lime juice

Soy Sauce
6 tablespoons soy sauce
1 tablespoon sugar
1 tablespoon chopped coriander

low to prepare
. Combine the ingredients from each sauce separately and place into small erving dishes.

. Prepare all seafood and drizzle with oil prior to cooking.

. Place prawns on BBQ for about 2 minutes, add fish for 3 minutes and then add quid. Turn over to brown other side & remove from heat once cooked.

. Depending on the thickness of the fish you may need to leave it on the BBQ for nother few minutes.

. Serve with dipping sauces and steamed or fried rice and or salad.

ecommended Beverage
n Australian crisp white wine like a Riesling-Sauvignon Blanc-Marsanne blend.

Recipe sponsored by Le Tigre de Papier

FISH AMOK
Amok Trey

Nothing characterizes Cambodian cuisine like fish amok! The popularity of this fish curry, which is typically wrapped in a banana leaf, can be adapted to include chicken, tofu and other meats. **Serves 4.**

Ingredients
4 large fish fillets (firm, white, non bony fillets recommended)
2 cups coconut cream
2 cups cabbage or spinach
1 tablespoon lemongrass, minced
1 tablespoon galangal,(or ginger) minced
1 teaspoon turmeric (fresh or powdered)
4 large kaffir lime leaves (extra for garnish)
4 cloves garlic, minced
2 large eggs, beaten
1 teaspoon salt
1 teaspoon sugar
2 teaspoons fish sauce
1 teaspoon shrimp paste
2 teaspoons dry red pepper paste (or red curry paste)

How to prepare
1. Mix the lemongrass, galangal, turmeric, garlic, salt, sugar, fish sauce, shrimp paste and red pepper paste together and set to one side.

2. Chop the fish into bite sized pieces and cover in above mixture. Add eggs to fish and stir until covered.

3. Line bowl with cabbage or spinach and add fish mixture. Place bowl in pan covered in water and cook in hot oven for about 10 minutes (until fish is firm and cooked. The bowl can also be placed in a large streamer to cook.

4. Top with coconut cream and kaffir lime leaves and steam for another 10 minutes. Serve with steamed rice.

Recommended Beverage
A Chillean round and fresh white wine like unoaky Chardonnay.

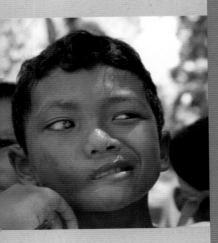

Recipe sponsored by Sugar Palm

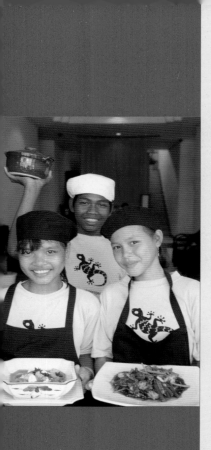

TAMARIND SEAFOOD CURRY
Machu Kreoung Samot Kari

Have your friends raving about your cooking expertise with this tasty seafood curry explosion, it will leave them begging you for the recipe. **Serves 4.**

Ingredients

450g or ½ kilo of seafood (white fish, squid, shrimp/prawns)
2 medium eggplants, cut into cubes
1 tablespoon dried tamarind
1 large onion, sliced
1 medium sweet potato, cubed
1 ¾ cups coconut milk
5 tablespoons chicken stock powder
1 teaspoon salt
2 teaspoons brown sugar
2 tablespoons fish sauce
2 pieces star anis
1 cinnamon stick
2 tablespoons coconut cream
2 tablespoons vegetable oil

Curry paste
1 stalk lemongrass
1 ½ tablespoons turmeric
1 ½ tablespoons fresh galangal (or ginger)
2 garlic cloves
2 shallots
2 lime leaves
1 red chilli, chopped finely

How to prepare

1. Clean seafood (de-shell, de-bone, de-vein) and if using fish/squid cut into thick cubes, place in a bowl to one side.

2. Pound the curry paste ingredients in a mortar & pestle or blend in a food processor until it turns into a smooth paste. Set to one side.

3. Heat the oil in a large wok/frypan on medium heat, add the onion, sweet potato, egg plant, curry paste and stir for about 4 minutes, then add about a ¼ of the coconut milk, sugar, salt, star anis, cinnamon stick and fish sauce and stir until combined.

4. After about 3 minutes, add the seafood and stir. Pour in the rest of the coconut milk, stock powder and tamarind and simmer for 5 minutes.

5. Remove from heat & dribble coconut cream on top and serve with steamed rice.

Recommended Beverage
A chilled Californian buttery white wine like a Chardonnay.

37

SEAFOOD & KAMPOT PEPPER STIRFRY
Char Samot Mrik Kechey

This sizzling seafood stir-fry with mixed vegetables is one of Cambodia's specialty recipes. Peppercorns from Kampot province have an excellent reputation for quality, their intense taste and pungency. If Kampot pepper is not available any peppercorns will do. **Serves 4**

Ingredients

16 medium sized fresh prawns/shrimps, shelled and de-veined
2 medium sized tubes of squid/calamari, sliced into rings
1 medium green capsicum (pepper) sliced thinly
1 medium red capsicum (pepper) sliced thinly
3 ½ tablespoons green Kampot peppercorns
1 cup of chicken or fish stock
3 tablespoons fresh basil, diced
2 tablespoons fresh coriander, diced
4 spring onion

3 tablespoons cooking oil
3 cloves garlic, minced
1 tablespoon sugar
1 tablespoon oyster sauce
2 tablespoons soy sauce
1 teaspoon fish sauce
½ cup water
2 tablespoons cornflour

How to prepare

1. De-shell and de-vein prawns and cut squid/calamari into thick cubes.

2. Combine sugar, oyster sauce, soy sauce, chopped coriander and fish sauce together and set to one side.

3. Heat oil in frypan/wok to a medium heat and add garlic, capsicums and peppercorns, stir for 5 minutes. Add squid and cook for about 2 minutes then add the shrimp and cook for a further 2 minutes.

4. Stir in the sauce mixture, allow to sizzle for 1 minute before adding in the chicken stock, continue cooking for about 2 minutes

5. Combine the water and the corn flour together, stir until smooth and add into the seafood mixture. Stir until combined and sauce thickens for about 2 minutes.

6. Remove from heat and add spring onion as garnish and serve with steamed rice.

Recommended Beverage

A spicy Spanish sunny white wine like a Parellada.

CRAB & BANANA BLOSSOM CURRY
Kari Kdam Troyong Cheik

his scrumptious Crab Curry will tantalise you with its blend of flavours and goes well with steamed
ce or hot crusty bread. If you can't find banana blossoms substitute water chestnuts for an extra
unch. **Serves 2.**

ngredients

medium sized sea crabs
cup smoked fish
cup coconut cream
cups coconut milk
teaspoon salt
teaspoon palm sugar (or brown sugar)
tablespoon fish sauce
tablespoons lime juice
tablespoon mint leaves, chopped
tablespoon basil leaves, chopped
banana blossom (substitute ½ cup water chestnuts, thinly sliced)

Curry paste

2 stalks lemongrass
1 tablespoon turmeric (or dried turmeric)
1 tablespoon galangal (or substitute ginger)
3 cloves garlic
1 teaspoon red chilli
1 tablespoon oyster sauce

ow to prepare

. Clean crabs and cut into quarters and prepare the smoked fish by pounding it in a mortar.

. Mix together the salt, sugar, fish sauce, lime juice, mint and basil together and set to one side.

. Blend all curry paste ingredients in a mixer or with a pestle & mortar until a thick paste forms.

. Pour the coconut cream into a pan over low heat until it starts to bubble, then stir in the curry paste.
ook for a further 3-5 minutes until it has a strong aromatic smell.

. Add in the crabs and cook for 8-10 minutes depending on the size of the crabs. Increase the heat
nd add the coconut milk. Stir until the mixture begins to boil. Blend in the banana blossom, smoked
sh, rest of the seasoning and stir until combined.

. Remove from heat and serve in a large bowl with steamed rice. Dollop with coconut cream.

ecommended Beverage

feisty French fresh white wine from Alsace like a Riesling.

41

CHICKEN

Chickens are kept by more than 80% of rural families, mainly for their egg production but more often than not they end up on the dining table.

One of the fascinating sights in Cambodia is the numerous ways chickens are transported to the markets; huge bunches of them tied to motorcycles, bicycles, trucks and boats. Once upon a time chickens were used during the marriage ceremony, - the man had to give the girl's family a minimum of "a chicken" as a bridal dowry.

FRESH CHICKEN SPRING ROLLS
Nhaem Sach Moan

Rice Paper Rolls are fantastic, they're healthy, tasty and a fabulous fresh snack. For a vegetarian option, you can use tofu instead of chicken. **Makes 12**.

Ingredients
1 carrot-grated
3 tablespoons bean sprouts
2 chicken fillets sliced finely
2 tablespoons oil
12 basil leaves
12 coriander leaves
½ lettuce torn into medium size pieces
1 teaspoon sesame oil
1 cup rice noodles soaked in hot water to soften
12 rice paper wrappers
2 tablespoons spring onion
1 tablespoon peanuts

How to prepare
1. Lightly fry the chicken fillets in a hot pan with oil, about 7 minutes. Put to one side to cool. Once cool, finely slice the chicken into thin strips.

2. Mix all vegetables, chicken, noodles together with sesame oil and divide into 12 equal portions.

3. Fill a large, shallow dish with warm water and soak a rice paper wrapper until softened (a few seconds at the most). Carefully transfer the wrapper to a dinner plate. Place one portion of the filling on the lower half of the wrapper.

4. Fold the lower edge of the wrapper up and lightly snuggle it around the filling. Fold in the left and right sides of the wrapper toward the center and roll cigar-style toward the upper edge.

5. Cut roll in half on a diagonal angle and place on an attractive serving dish. Repeat with the remaining wrappers and fillings.

6. Serve with spring onions and peanuts as garnish and dipping sauce.

Recommended Beverage
A chilled light and tangy French Bordeaux white wine.

Dipping Sauce
½ cup lime juice
¼ cup fish sauce
½ cup hot water
¼ cup granulated sugar
4 cloves garlic peeled and chopped finely
1 small chilli pepper, trimmed, seeded and finely chopped

How to prepare
Mix all ingredients together in a jar with a tight-fitting lid. Shake vigorously and allow to stand for at least hour or overnight if possible. Serve in a shallow dish with the Fresh Rice Paper Chicken rolls. Alternatively you can use a sweet chilli sauce for dipping.

CHICKEN BANANA BLOSSOM SALAD
Nhoam Trohyong Cheik Sach Moan

This spicy chicken and banana blossom salad combines the tantalizing tangy flavours of Cambodia and can be used as both a main meal or as a side salad. If you can't find fresh banana blossoms, you can substitute the canned variety. **Serves 4.**

Ingredients

banana blossom
large chicken breasts
lemon juiced
cups water
cup loosely packed mint leaves
cup loosely packed basil leaves
cup bean sprouts
medium red capsicum, thinly sliced
½ cup peanuts, roasted and coarsely ground
/3 cup dressing for salad (see below)

Dressing for salad (Tuk Trey)
1/4 cup water
½ cup sugar
1 garlic clove
1 small shallot
2 tablespoons fish sauce
5 teaspoons lime juice
1 teaspoon salt
1 red chilli
Extra lemon or lime

How to prepare

1. Fill a large bowl ½ way to the top with water and the juice of 1 lemon. Set to one side.

2. Remove the tough outer layer of the banana blossom, along with the undeveloped "baby" bananas and discard. Slice the young, pale, pinkish leaves into very thin strips. Place into lemon water to prevent them from turning black.

3. In a medium saucepan, bring the water to a boil. Add in the chicken breasts and simmer for 10 to 15 minutes, until the meat is cooked. Remove the chicken from the pan, cool it slightly, then shred the meat with your fingers.

4. In a large salad bowl, toss all the vegetables, mint and basil together with the chicken. Setting aside a handful for garnish, mix in the ground peanuts. Add dressing and toss. Sprinkle with remaining peanuts and serve immediately.

Dressing for salad

1. In a small saucepan, bring the water to the boil and add the sugar, stirring to dissolve. Allow to cool.

2. Pound the garlic, chilli and shallots into small pieces, then stir into syrupy water. Add the remaining ingredients and stir.

Recommended Beverage
An Argentinean light fruity white wine like a Viognier.

47

STEAMED CHICKEN WITH LEMONGRASS SOUP

Chemhay Moan Sleek Krey

This soup has a tantalising variation of flavours that you and your family and friends will really enjoy. If you cannot locate fresh galangal then you can substitute it with fresh ginger. **Serves 2.**

Ingredients
2 boneless chicken breasts, skinned and diced
4 cups chicken stock
3 stalks fresh lemongrass, mashed
4 garlic cloves, chopped
2 teaspoons fish sauce
1 teaspoon fresh galangal or substitute with ginger
1 teaspoon black pepper
4 spring onions, chopped
2 tablespoons basil, chopped
juice of half a lime
1 teaspoon chilli paste (to taste)
1 teaspoon chopped coriander
5 kaffir lime leaves

How to prepare
1. Put stock, lemon grass, garlic, fish sauce, galangal and pepper in a large saucepan and bring to the boil.

2. Add the chicken, mixing well and cook for 10 minutes, skimming off any white froth which forms.

3. Place the spring onions, basil lemon juice, chilli paste, coriander and lime leaves in a large serving bowl and mix well.

4. To serve, pour the soup over the onion mixture in the serving bowl, mix well and serve immediately.

Recommended Beverage
An Australian crisp and light white wine like a Sauvignon Blanc.

Recipe sponsored by Earthwalkers

BBQ CHICKEN WITH FRIED RICE
Bai Char Moan Ang

The all-time favourite of the Green Gecko kids, the tender chicken and delicious fried rice will leave your guests queuing up for seconds and thirds. **Serves 4**

Ingredients
4 large chicken thighs
2 tablespoons ginger, finely chopped
2 tablespoons lemongrass, finely chopped
2 tablespoons coriander root
2 tablespoons pepper
1 tablespoon sugar
1 ½ tablespoon curry powder
2 tablespoons soy sauce
1 red capsicum, sliced
Spring onion for garnish
4 slices tomato for garnish
1 lime sliced into quarters

Sauce
1 tablespoon of red chilli, diced
1 tablespoon garlic, diced
2 teaspoons salt
2 teaspoons sugar
½ cup brown vinegar

How to prepare
1. Mix all the ingredients in a pot and simmer over low heat, stir occasionally until it becomes a smooth syrup, about 10 minutes. Remove and set to one side.

2. Blend ginger, lemongrass and coriander and coat over the chicken fillets.

3. Combine soy sauce, sugar, pepper and curry powder and pour over chicken. Leave the chicken to marinate in the fridge for at least 1 hour.

Recommended Beverage
A full bodied and well balanced sweet malt Ale.

Fried Rice
1 tablespoon peanut oil (or vegetable oil)
6 cloves garlic, minced
1 medium onion, chopped
1 cup oyster mushrooms, sliced
1 small red capsicum, chopped
1 medium tomato, chopped
2 teaspoons fish sauce (or to taste)
1 teaspoon soy sauce
2 eggs lightly beaten
3 cups of cooked Jasmine rice

Fried Rice
1. Heat the oil in a frypan and when the oil begins to sizzle, add the onion and cook until transparent.

2. Add the capsicum, stir for about 3 minutes until softened, add garlic and mushrooms and cook for a further 3 minutes.

3. Add the cooked rice, breaking it up with your fingers, keep stirring for 4-5 minutes until mixed through. Mix in the eggs and stir until cooked. Add the tomato, fish & soy sauce and cook for 1 minute. Place lid on the top to keep warm.

5. Char-grill the chicken over medium heat until cooked.

6. Combine the chicken and fried rice on a plate and garnish with tomato slices and lime wedges.

51

RED CHICKEN CURRY
Kari Sach Moan

This aromatic chicken curry dish will delightfully linger on your taste buds and is distinctly reminiscent of the spicy fresh tastes and smells of Cambodia. **Serves 2.**

Ingredients
2 large chicken fillets, cubed
2 onions, cubed
2 cups coconut milk
5 teaspoons fish sauce
5 teaspoons sugar
1 teaspoon salt
5 teaspoons curry powder
4 tablespoons peanuts, chopped
6 tablespoons vegetable oil

Spices
2 tablespoons fresh galangal (or ginger), chopped finely
2 teaspoons turmeric, if fresh chop finely
3 lime leaves, sliced thinly
2 lemongrass stalks, chopped finely
3 cloves garlic, chopped finely
3 spring onions (shallots), chopped finely
2 teaspoons dried chilli
2 teaspoons shrimp paste

How to prepare
1. Combine galangal, turmeric, lime leaves, lemongrass, garlic, shallots, dried chilli and shrimp paste together.

2. To cook the curry, place a pot over medium high heat and add the oil. When the oil is hot, add the spice mixture and sauté for about 3 minutes until fragrant.

3. Add onions and continue cooking for another 3 minutes. Add the chicken pieces and continue to sauté until the meat is well covered with the spice mixture.

4. Now add the rest of the ingredients and simmer until the chicken & onions are tender, about 5 minutes. Taste the sauce to make sure the curry is well flavoured and add more chilli if you would like to spice it up.

5. Serve the curry in a bowl with steamed rice.

For an exotic serving suggestion spoon curry into lotus flower petals for bite sized mouthfuls.

Recommended Beverage
An aromatic crisp and refreshing Chilean white wine like a Gewurztraminer.

SPICY CHICKEN STIRFRY
Moan Char Kdeow

Spice up (or down) this very popular delicious chicken dish according to how hot you like it!!! This yummy dish also allows you to substitute other types of meat. **Serves 4.**

Ingredients
4 chicken fillets, cut into bite size pieces
2 medium onions, chopped
2 cups chicken stock
2 tablespoons cooking oil
½ teaspoon sugar (add more for sweeter flavour)
1 tablespoon fish sauce
2 tablespoons soy sauce
2 cloves garlic, minced
2 stalks lemongrass, mashed
2 small red chillis, minced (more for extra hot)
1 teaspoon turmeric, mashed (or powdered)
Basil leaves (approx 6-8 per person)

How to prepare
1. Heat fry pan until hot, pour in oil, garlic and onions and cook until slightly browned.

2. Add chicken fillets & stir for about 3 minutes until chicken is golden brown.

3. Combine chilli, lemongrass, turmeric then add spice mixture to chicken and stir until chicken is coated.

4. Add chicken stock, soy sauce, fish sauce and sugar. Simmer 10 minutes until the chicken is cooked.

5. Add basil and stir for a further 1 minute.

6.Serve hot with steamed rice.

Recommended Beverage
A popular Chilean light bodied red wine.

PORK

Cambodians are champion motorcycle riders and motorbikes are used to transport all types of things and pigs are no exception.

Its not uncommon to see huge pigs laying catatonically on the back of a moto as it passes you by.

57

SWEET & SPICY PORK RIBS
Chemney Chruk Chouaem

Finger licking good or 'Lahore' (beautiful in Cambodian) these ribs make a great snack or as a delicious main with rice. The ribs can either be cooked in their rack or sliced into pieces. **Serves 4.**

Ingredients
1 ½ kilos pork spare ribs, cut into bite size cubes
3 cloves garlic, finely minced
2 spring onions (scallions), finely chopped
4 tablespoons soy sauce
2 tablespoons honey
2 teaspoons brown sugar
3 tablespoons tomato paste
1 teaspoon dried chilli
2 tablespoons lime juice
½ cup water
2 tablespoons vegetable oil
2 tablespoons spring onions, chopped

How to prepare
1. Mix all marinade ingredients together in a large bowl.

2. Add pork ribs and toss to coat. Cover and marinate in the refrigerator for a few hours.

3. Place ribs on a foil-lined baking sheet and bake in a medium hot oven for about 40 to 50 minutes, turning over every 20 minutes, until tender, being careful not to overcook.

4. Serve the ribs on their own, sprinkled with spring onions, with a salad or with rice.

Recommended Beverage
A strong dark ale with a sweet malty flavour.

CAMBODIAN PORK COLESLAW
Spey Sach Chruk Chrouk

This light and refreshing dish is an explosion of tastes and sensations its not only crunchy and tangy its also really really good for you. If you are having difficulty finding lotus flower root you can use chestnuts as a substitute. **Serves 2.**

Ingredients

large pork steaks
tablespoons vegetable oil
cups cabbage, sliced finely
medium sized onion
medium sized carrots, sliced into matchsticks
slices of lotus flower root
 green/red & yellow capsicum, sliced into matchsticks
teaspoon fish sauce
5 sweet basil leaves
teaspoons roasted black sesame seeds
tablespoons roasted peanuts, chopped
ices of lime

Coconut dressing:

2 tablespoons vegetable oil
2 spring onions/shallots, chopped finely
3 cloves garlic, chopped finely
2 teaspoons ginger, chopped finely
2 tablespoons sweet chilli sauce
1 teaspoon sugar
3 tablespoons coconut oil (or olive oil)
2 tablespoons lime juice

How to prepare

. First prepare the coconut dressing by sauteing the shallots, garlic and ginger in oil until soft, about 3 inutes over a medium heat

. Add chilli sauce, fish sauce and sugar and cook for a further 2 minutes.

. Take off heat, cool slightly and then add lime juice and coconut oil. Place to one side.

. Rinse lotus roots and cut near the "necks," discarding the top section. Rinse, peel and slice crosswise to 1/8-inch-thick slices. Submerge in water with some lemon juice and leave to one side.

. Slice the pork into long strips and place into hot pan with vegetable oil. After 2 minutes add the onions nd lotus flower (removed from water) and cook for a further 3 minutes.

. Mix the cabbage, carrots, basil and capsicums together and place on a serving plate.

. Layer pork, onions and lotus flower onto the top, pour over coconut dressing, sprinkle on peanuts and esame seeds.

Recommended Beverage
. dry but zesty Chardonnay from America's famous Napa Valley.

61

PORK & PUMPKIN STIRFRY
Char Sach Chruk Misour

The pork and pumpkin partnership with a hint of cardamom is a marriage of flavours made in heaven. **Serves 4.**

Ingredients
4 pork fillets, sliced
1 medium pumpkin, sliced into sticks
1/4 cup vegetable oil
1/2 medium sized green capsicum (pepper)
1/2 medium sized red capsicum (pepper)
1/2 medium sized yellow capsicum (pepper)
1/4 cup fish sauce
1 1/2 tablespoons sugar
1/2 ground cardamom
1/2 teaspoon black pepper
5 garlic cloves, smashed and coarsely chopped
3 sprigs spring onions (scallions), thinly sliced

How to prepare
1. Combine the fish sauce, sugar, cardamom and pepper and set to one side.

2. Slice both the pork and pumpkin into similar sized sticks. At the same time also slice the capsicums into thin slices.

3. Heat the oil in a frypan/wok over medium-high heat. Add the pumpkin and cook for 5 minutes before adding the garlic, cook until the garlic is a golden brown, about a further 2 minutes.

4. Stir in the pork and continue to cook for a further 2 minutes.

5. Then add the capsicums and the sauce mixture and continue stir-frying for about 3 minutes or until the pork is well cooked.

6. Add the spring onions, stir well, and remove from heat and serve over rice.

Recommended Beverage
A chilled dry Semignon Chardonnay from New Zealand.

PORK NOODLE SALAD

Nhoam Sach Chruk Misour

This is the simplest pork and noodle recipe and is also one of Cambodia's favourites, often eaten at breakfast time. You'll be amazed at how good this is. The pork can be substituted for chicken or tofu. **Serves 2**

Ingredients

2 medium sized pork steaks, diced
2 cups rice noodles
1 cup cabbage, sliced finely
2 medium sized carrots, finely sliced
¼ green capsicum, sliced
½ red capsicum, sliced
½ yellow capsicum, sliced
1 small cucumber, grated
4 tablespoons peanuts, crushed
Fresh basil for garnish
Extra chilli (if you prefer a hotter taste)

4 tablespoons sugar
1 teaspoon salt
3 tablespoons fish sauce
3 cloves garlic, finely chopped
2 tablespoons fresh lime juice
1 teaspoon dried chicken stock
2 tablespoons oil

How to prepare

1. Heat pan with oil and when hot add in bite sized pork pieces for about 5 minutes turning oven to ensure pork is evenly cooked. After 5 minutes add in the capsicum and fry for a further 2 minutes.

2. Remove from heat when pork turns to an even golden brown colour and is cooked in the middle.

3. Combine peanuts, sugar, fish sauce, chicken stock, lime juice, salt and garlic tighter and mix until combined. Add cooked pork and stir until coated.

4. Add glassy noodles to a pot of boiling water for one minute. Drain excess water and place noodles into a bowl with cabbage and cucumber. Stir until combined then add the pork mixture.

5. Place onto serving plate, garnish with basil and extra chilli

Recommended Beverage

A fabulous chilled French wine from the Loire Valley

BEEF

Every year the Royal Ploughing Ceremony takes place in which 2 hungry royal cows are served seven golden trays, each one topped with rice, rice wine, maize, water, sesame, grass and beans.

What the cows eat or don't eat predicts the upcoming year's harvest. Feasting on rice is a good sign, but drinking the rice wine instead of the water could predict a drought!

BEEF, LEMONGRASS & GREEN BEAN STIRFRY

Char Sach Ko, Sendaich Kour

Lemongrass is one of those wondrous herbs that is widely used in many Cambodian dishes. It is renowned for its aromatic citrus flavour scented with a trace of ginger. Lemongrass & beef is a terrific partnership and this delicious main meal is both aromatic and mouth watering. **Serves 2**

Ingredients

2 medium size beef tenderloins
2 medium onions, sliced
2 tablespoons fish sauce
1 tablespoon oyster sauce
1 tablespoon sugar
11 green beans, sliced
4 tablespoons water

2 medium red capsicums, sliced
2 lemongrass stalks, chopped finely
¼ cup roasted peanuts, chopped
1 teaspoon salt
3 tablespoons curry paste
2 tablespoons oil
1 tablespoon corn flour

How to prepare

1. Slice the beef into strips and place to one side. Heat a wok or fry pan to a high heat and add oil and beef, cook for about 5 minutes.

2. Add capsicum, onion, oyster sauce, fish sauce, salt, sugar, curry paste, lemongrass and stir quickly for about 2 minutes.

3. Mix water and corn flour together and once smooth add to the pan and stir through to ensure a thick consistency. Add a little more water for a thinner consistency.

4. Add sliced beans and cook for a further 2 minutes. Remove from pan and serve with steamed rice.

Recommended Beverage

A South African full bodied red wine such as a Pinotage.

Recipe sponsored by La Residence d' Angkor

BEEF & MUSHROOM SOUP
Samlor Sach Ko Sut

This soup is perfect any time especially in cold weather. Add diced potatoes for a heartier stew. **Serves 2**.

Ingredients
1 ½ cups minced beef
1 cup oyster mushrooms, chopped roughly
2 medium sized onions, sliced
4 cloves garlic, chopped
2 tablespoons vegetable oil
2 cups beef stock
1 cup water
2 tablespoons soy sauce
2 teaspoons pepper
2 tablespoons mint, chopped
2 teaspoons parsley, chopped

How to prepare
1. In a pot add the oil and sauté the onions and garlic over a medium heat until golden brown, about 4 minutes.

2. Add the minced beef and cook for a further 4 minutes, stirring to make sure the beef is evenly cooking.

3. Add the beef stock, soy sauce and water and boil for about 6 minutes.

4. Add in the mushrooms, pepper, ¾ of the mint, cook for a further 2-3 minutes and take off the heat.

5. Prior to serving sprinkle parsley and mint on the top

Recommended Beverage
A New Zealand well balanced red wine like a Pinot Noir.

Recipe sponsored by Shinta Mani

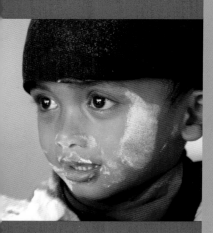

STIR-FRIED BEEF WITH NOODLES
Mee Char Sach Ko

This is a quick, easy to prepare and very tasty stirfry. Try blanching the veggies to make them a little softer before you stirfry them. **Serves 2**.

Ingredients
2 medium size beef tenderloin, sliced thinly
2 medium onions, sliced
1 cup button, oyster or shiitake mushrooms, sliced
½ cup cabbage, sliced
½ cup in-season greens (i.e. spinach, broccoli)
3 medium sized carrots, sliced
2 tablespoons vegetable oil
4 tablespoons soy sauce
2 tablespoons water
2 tablespoons oyster sauce
1 teaspoon sugar
1 ½ cup thin egg noodles
Small dish dried/fresh chilli

How to prepare
1. Heat a wok or frypan to a high heat and add oil beef and onions until onions soften, about 4 minutes.

2. Add carrots and cook for a further 2 minutes. Combine oyster sauce, soy sauce, water and sugar, together.

3. Add to beef and stir. Then toss in the cabbage, local greens and mushrooms and stir through beef. Cook for no more than 2 minutes and lower down heat to low.

4. Add noodles to a pot of boiling water for one minute. Drain excess water and toss noodles through beef mixture. Serve with chlli on the side for more spice.

Recommended Beverage
An Australian powerful full bodied red wine like a blend of Shiraz Cabernet.

CAMBODIAN BEEF LOK LAK
Sach Ko Lok Lak

This is a very popular dish in Cambodia and involves 3 separate dishes of a marinade, sauce and a dipping sauce. It is traditionally served with rice and a fried egg on the top. "Chgnayn!!" (very delicious!!). **Serves 2**

Ingredients

2 large prime beef fillets
1 medium sized onion
2 eggs
2 tomatoes
3 tablespoons vegetable oil
8 teaspoons freshly squeezed lime juice
Lettuce (for garnish)

2 tablespoons garlic, chopped finely
2 tablespoons soy sauce
2 tablespoons oyster sauce
2 teaspoons salt
1 teaspoon pepper
½ teaspoon sugar
4 teaspoons black pepper

How to prepare

1. Thinly slice the onion and tomatoes into rings. Garnish each plate with a layer of lettuce, onion & finally place the tomato on top. Place to one side until ready.

2. To make the marinade mix together the garlic, soy sauce & salt & pepper.

3. Slice the beef fillet into strips, add the marinade & coat. Leave in the fridge to marinate for 10 minutes.

4. To make the sauce mix together the oyster sauce, sugar & oil.

5. Heat a tablespoon of extra oil into a wok or large frying pan. Wait until the oil is hot and add marinated beef. Stir fry until brown, then add the sauce & warm through.

6. In a separate frying pan fry two eggs. When eggs are cooked, serve the beef on top of the salad & place one egg on top of each dish.

7. To make the dipping pepper sauce, mix together the black pepper, 1 teaspoon salt & lime juice. Place in small dish for dipping.

8. Serve with either steamed rice or French Fries & eat & enjoy.

Recommended Beverage
A Spanish spicy and fruity red wine like a Garna Cha.

DESSERTS & DRINKS

Sweet dishes include sticky rice cakes and fruit pudding, and the abundance of fresh pineapple, mango, papaya and dragonfruit are enjoyed throughout the day.

The most popular local drink is water with a squeeze of lime and a dash of sugar syrup. The country's national beer, Angkor, is enjoyed by local people and tourists alike at $1 a pop, its hard to say no!

PUMPKIN CUSTARD PIE
Sangkya L'Peuv

This enjoyable combination of savory pumpkin and sweet custard is easy to make and when served will impress your guests.

Makes 10 small slices.

Ingredients
1 whole small pumpkin
8 egg yolks
1 cup sugar
1¾ cups coconut milk
1 teaspoon salt
1 vanilla pod

How to prepare
1. Cut a big hole in the top of the pumpkin and remove seeds from the inside. You can also use a ½ butternut pumpkin.

2. To prepare custard mixture, mix egg yolk, sugar, coconut milk and salt together in a bowl, whisk until thick, about 5 minutes.

3. Pour into the pumpkin through the hole.

4. To cook the pumpkin place into a high sided pan, half filled with water and steam until cook, about 30 minutes in a hot oven.

5. To serve, cut into slices and serve with coconut ice cream

**Recipe
sponsored by
Raffles Grand Hotel d'Angkor**

Recommended Beverage
A French sweet wine like a Cotes de Montravel.

BANANA SLICE
Cheik K'Tih

This banana pudding is a combination of Cambodians two most popular fruits, banana and coconut. It is versatile enough to add in different spices, dried fruits and nuts if you want to be more creative.

Makes 18 slices.

Ingredients
3 medium sized ripe bananas
2 eggs
¾ cup rice flour
¾ cup dark palm sugar (or substitute brown sugar)
1 cup coconut milk
1 pinch salt
2 egg yolks (for glazing)

How to prepare
1. Mash the bananas with a fork.

2. Add the rice flour, then the salt and palm sugar and mix together.

3. Then add the coconut milk and whole eggs and stir until combined.

4. Pour into a baking tray and bake 10 minutes in a medium oven.

5. Mix the yolks together and brush the top of the mixture.

6. Bake for a further 10 minutes.

7. Serve cold with sliced banana or ice cream

Recommended Beverage
A light and fruity French wine from Alsace like a Gewurztraminer.

**Recipe
sponsored by
Hotel de la Paix**

COCONUT RICE PUDDING
Dong Bai Treip

This yummy slice can be served as both a snack or as a dessert. Depending on the type of coconut milk and rice used could change the outcome, but will taste just as delicious.
Makes 24 slices.

Ingredients
1 cup short or round-grain rice
2 cups coconut milk
1 cup milk
½ cup water
1 large strip lime rind, cut into small strips
¼ cup palm (or brown) sugar
¼ cup of butter, cut into small cubes
2 teaspoons cinnamon
1 teaspoon ground star anise
½ vanilla pod (or 2 teaspoons)
fresh or stewed fruit

How to prepare
1. Mix the rice with the coconut milk, milk, water, lime rind and sugar.

2. Pour the rice mixture into a lightly-greased shallow oven-proof dish and scatter the top with butter. Bake in a hot oven for about 30 minutes.

3. Stir the rice mixture well, add the cinnamon, vanilla and ground star anise, return to the oven and cook for a further 60 80 minutes or until almost all the milk has been absorbed and a golden brown skin has baked on the top of the pudding.

4. Cover the top of the pudding with foil if it starts to brown too much towards the end of the cooking time.

Serve the pudding warm or chilled with fresh or stewed fruit

Recommended Beverage
An aromatic German white wine from Rheinessen like a Riesling.

Recipe sponsored by NEDO

MANGO SHAKE
Teuk Kelok Svaytum

veryone will love this creamy, delicious shake which is a great way to kick
art your morning or to cool down on a hot summer day. Other fruits can
e used in place of the mango. **Serves 4.**

ngredients

medium sized mangoes   4 cups milk
tablespoons sugar   ¼ cup water
2 ice cubes   sprigs of mint

ow to prepare

. Dissolve the sugar in the water over low heat, and allow to cool.

. Remove the skin from the mangoes and cut away the flesh from the pip.

. Place mango pulp, milk, sugar water and ice cubes into the blender,
nd whiz until smooth.

LIME JUICE
Teuk Krouch Cmar

his is one of Cambodia's most popular non alcoholic drinks and is just
e thing when unexpected guests drop by, or on a hot summer day. This
ecipe is not only easy and simple to prepare but your guests will be
equesting a top-up. **Serves 4.**

ngredients

1/2 cup freshly squeezed lime juice
cups cold water   1 cup sugar
ce cubes   4 lime slice twists
mint sprigs

ow to prepare

. Mix lime juice, water and sugar. Serve over ice in tall glasses and
garnish with lime slice twists and mint.

2. Also, the ice cubes can be processed in a blender or food processor
with the mixture to make a delicious lime slush.

TAMARIND TEA
Mpel Tai

Tamarind tea, a refreshing drink with a
subtle, sweet and tangy flavour, is made
by combining the tamarind seed pods
with water and sugar. **Serves 4.**

Ingredients
4 tablespoons of tamarind paste
4 cups of boiling water
sugar or honey (to taste)

How to prepare
1. Bring water to a boil and pour into
cup or mug.

2. Add 1 tablespoon of tamarind paste to
each cup and stir until dissolved.

3. Stir in sugar or honey to taste.

4. Serve hot or refrigerate and serve over
ice.

Other variations: a few spoonfuls of lime
juice, cinnamon, or grated ginger may be
combined with the tamarind pulp before
the water is added.

CAMBODIAN HERBS & SPICES

The Khmer people enjoy spices that are mild and allow other herbs and flavors such as ginger, lemongrass and tamarind to create a distinct yet simple taste to their salads, soups, meat and sauces. Many of their recipes require the blending of specific spices such as cardamom, star anise, cloves, cinnamon, nutmeg, ginger and turmeric to create an aromatic paste.

Local aromatic herbs such as lemongrass, garlic and coriander (cilantro) are used generously, and slightly more unique herbs such as galangal and kaffir lime leaves give Khmer cookery a distinctive taste. Lemongrass can often be found in people's gardens, due to its popularity in cooking and basil is widely used to both add flavour and as a finishing touch to presentation.

Spices are very popular for adding depth to a dish, and in particular cardamom, ginger and turmeric give dishes warmth and zest.

chilli
an essential part of a Cambodian meal which adds both colour and spice to many dishes. Generally served on the side and used according to taste.

lotus roots
has a crisp, crunchy texture with a subtle sweet flavour and is added to soups, salads and stir-fry's. You can substitute for celery, water chestnuts or Jerusalem artichokes

banana blossom
the outer leaves are removed as well as the banana blossoms to reveal a pinkish white heart. The heart is then chopped and used predominately in salads. To prevent browning, soak the chopped heart in lemon or lime water.

sweet basil
has a mint like zesty flavour which is more often used in stir-fry or as a garnish

mint
one of the most common ingredients found in Cambodian salads, it has an intense spearmint flavour.

lemongrass
is an intensely fragrant stalk that has a tangy lemon flavour. The thick lower end of the stem, nearest the root, is the edible part. Discard the outer leaves until you reach the inner core

saw leaf
related to the coriander family although with a more mild flavour, saw leaf gets it name from its serrated leaves, which loosely resemble a saw

coriander powder
has a distinct sweet lemony flavour and can be purchased as a powder or as seeds (to grind).

black sesame
have a stronger more earthy flavour than the more common white sesame seeds.

black kampot pepper
with its slightly eucalyptus peppery punch is hard to find but is known as one of the worlds finest peppers.

white cardamom
is milder than the green variety and has a delicate flavour that goes well in Cambodia cuisine.

turmeric powder
is found in most curry powders and not only adds colour to your dish but has a subtle spicy flavour that also has many medicinal benefits.

white kampot pepper
is more subtle in flavour and aroma than black pepper due to the fact that it is ripe when picked.

turmeric
is a ground root related to ginger with a slightly bitter taste. The root is bright orange inside and produces a beautiful colour.

galangal root
resembles ginger in taste and appearance. It is ivory white and most often used in soups and stirfrys.

star anise
is a wonderful star shaped fruit with a powerful and liquorice-like aroma and taste.

kaffir lime leaves
have a luscious aroma and striking flavour. They are indispensable in many curry dishes which is one reason why Cambodian curries taste refreshingly unique.

coriander
or cilantro is a member of the parsley family used in salads, soups and stir-fry's or as a garnish.

TEAM SHINTA MANI

We were delighted when Tania Palmer at Green Gecko contacted us and invited us to participate in the recipe creation for the cookbook. Our two organisations have a lot in common with our core purpose is to help break the cycle of poverty and create opportunities for learning and employment in young under privileged Cambodians,

While Green Gecko helps the beggar children of Siem Reap, Shinta Mani provides free hospitality training for young at risk Cambodians, over the age of 18years. Our 9 month training programs for up to 28 students is funded by the hotel and by private individuals.

The students are selected by various local NGO's in consultation with the management of the school and are all struggling young Cambodians who have had a tough start in life. In fact several of Green Gecko's children are booked to come and attend our training program when they are old enough.

Our current 21 students enjoyed the opportunity to create a host of different recipes for the cookbook and found the interaction with the Green Gecko children very rewarding. The college rang with lots of laughter during the 4 day photo shoot.

Just about to graduate, these students who have learnt not just 16 culinary skills but other roles and positions within the hotel industry are looking forward to embarking on new permanent employment within Cambodia.

Besides paying no fees each student is paid a monthly stipend, uniforms, meals, study materials and a weekly supply of 4 kilograms of rice for their families until they graduate.

Our commitment and dedication to support the less fortunate community in Cambodia has changed many lives, supported many educations and brought a better future for Cambodia and its people.

So far to date (Shinta Mani opened in 2004) we have successfully trained 108 men and women who are now all working full time in restaurants, guesthouses and hotels across Cambodia.

Please check out our internet site for more information www.shintamani.com or pop in and ask for a tour of our school.

Chitra Vincent
General Manager
Shinta Mani

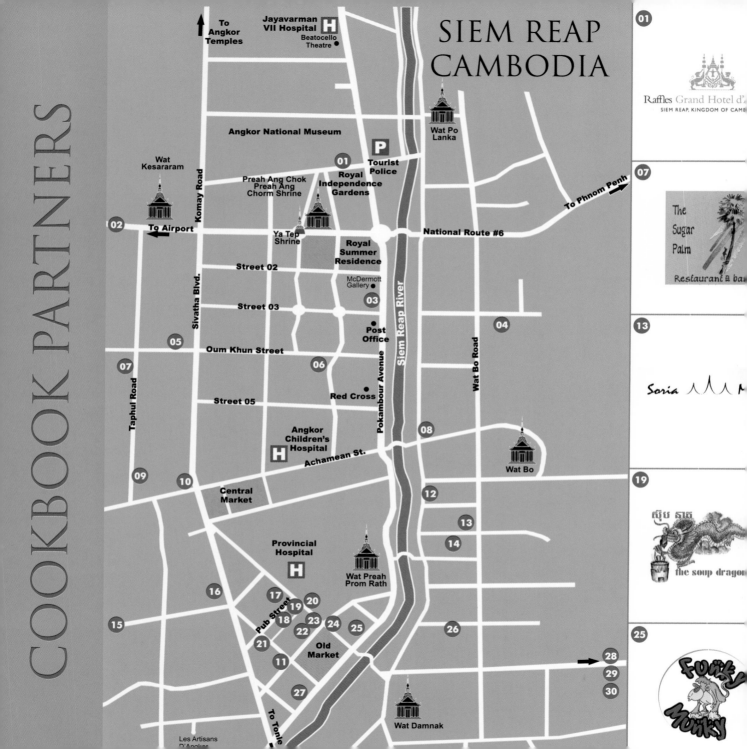

...walkers

03
FCC
PHNOM PENH · ANGKOR

04
TWO DRAGONS GUESTHOUSE & RESTAURANT

05
Abacus
Garden Restaurant & Bar

06
SHINTA MANI
Hotel and Institute of Hospitality

Résidence
Angkor
IENT-EXPRESS HOTELS
TRAINS & CRUISES

09
The Villa
Siem Reap
www.thevillasiemreap.com

10
HÔTEL DE LA PAIX
SIEM REAP

11
IVY
GUEST HOUSE & BAR
SIEM REAP

12
Chilli
SI-DANG winebar & restaurant

CELLIERS D'ASIE

...ders of our cookbook's
...he recommendations

15
MINISTRY OF SPICE
EST. 2007
SIEM REAP
KINGDOM OF CAMBODIA

16
Dead Fish
Siem Reap, Cambodia

17
Silk garden
Bar Restaurant

18
Le Tigre de Papier
and Cooking School

the blue pumpkin

21
Balcony Café

22

23
L Grand Café

24
THE WAREHOUSE
OLD MARKET · SIEM REAP · CAMBODIA

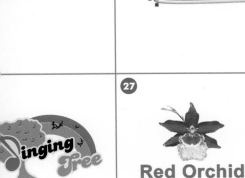
...inging Tree

27
Red Orchid
Restaurant & Bar

28
SYDNEY
Aqua

29
NEDO

30
green gecko
greengeckoproject.org

As resident's and restaurant owners in Siem Reap, it is impossible not to notice the effect that the Green Gecko Project has had on the streets. Less than a year ago, outside every bar and restaurant were hordes of unwashed and hungry children, hands outstretched to patrons and passers—by, many of them sleeping on the pavement just outside our doors. To see them today you can't imagine that they are the same children. From the beginning Tania and Rem's efforts and dedication made a difference; on behalf of the kids, their families and Siem Reap business owners, we salute you.

Trixie, Mac, Alex & Staff
Funky Munky Bar

GECKO MAIL

As a business, hug-a-bub is all about safety, security and nurturing. And Tania, as a business partner, is dedicated, generous and passionate. When Tania up and left Australia to act on feelings she had for the street children of Siem Reap, it was of little surprise to see what miracles she and Rem have been able to manifest.

While we miss her physical presence in our lives and our office, she is a total inspiration to us all. It has been a privilege to be a part of the Green Gecko Project from conception and to watch it all unfold. We are proud to support Tania financially so she and Rem can continue to be the beacons of light and hope they are to so many.

Suzanne Shahar
Director hugabub.com

"We all live our lives day-to-day and in doing so we often don't take time or give thought to the full impact of that which we do. I once read 'Everyone has a past which drives their future' & I believe these few words reflect the Green Gecko you have both created. You have provided hope & opportunity where previously there was none & the children of Green Gecko can only benefit from their experiences, education, & care you are providing them. As these children, & those to come, grow, Green Gecko will be perhaps the most singular influencing experience of their past & I have no doubt in my mind their futures will be so much brighter for your love & the opportunities you have created for them."

Doug South
Volunteer

street kids | siem reap | cambodia
greengeckoproject.org

93